Declarations

THAT

Empower
US

To Molly
Enjoy the journey
Blessings
David

DECLARATIONS
THAT
EMPOWER
US

DAVID CRONE

PUBLISHED BY:
MARK 16:15 INTERNATIONAL
6391 Leisure Town Road, Vacaville, California 95687

COVER DESIGN BY: Jared Teska
Teska Photography & Design
JaredTeskaPhotography.com

Printed in the United States of America
First Edition: May 2013

DEDICATION

This book is dedicated to those in the community of faith called The Mission. Never have I known such a prophetically tenacious group of people so willing to believe and declare until they see. They have shown me the way to live in faith, hope, and love.

CONTENTS

FOREWORD

In this powerful book, David Crone has tapped into the very heart of God for this new epoch season. *Declarations That Empower Us* unearths the power of our words for a new season. The average person today hears more bad news in one week than someone just 50 years ago would have heard in his or her entire lifetime. Without even realizing it, most Christians have been boiled in the oil of skepticism, pessimism, and negativism. This has resulted in faithless Christianity—unbelieving believers struggling through life carrying a deep sense of hopelessness and foreboding. Yet in the midst of this tumultuous age, God has seated us in heavenly places, empowering us to have timeless perspectives as well as supernatural solutions.

Metaphorically speaking, much of the Church has left the slave camp of Egypt only to find themselves stuck in an endless cycle of powerless living. Some have become so convinced that the abundant life Jesus promised is only apprehended in the "sweet by and by," leaving them in the hopeless "here and now."

Declarations That Empower Us is like the prince who kissed

13

Sleeping Beauty awake! It will awaken you into new dimensions in God. For some people, this book will shift the very foundation of what it means to come into agreement with the kingdom of Heaven and off the map of predictable living. It's only when we leave the shores of a monotonous existence and set sail for the Promised Land that we meet the Captain of the Host and discover the adventure of a lifetime.

Declarations That Empower Us is a training manual for God's reigning royalty. These declarations are dedicated to transforming our minds so that we can view life through God's eternal perspectives and bring hope to this desperate and dying planet. Every Christian needs to read this book! Without question, it will change your thinking and transform the world around you.

—Kris Vallotton
Leader, Bethel Church, Redding, California
Co-Founder of Bethel School of Supernatural Ministry
Author of nine books, including
The Supernatural Ways of Royalty and *Spirit Wars.*

Declarations can be dangerous
to life as you presently know it.
Please do not use with caution,
but with intentionality.

INTRODUCTION

Deborah and I have had the privilege of living among a community of believers known as The Mission for over twenty years. We have worked through many struggles in becoming what we now are. We faced difficulties and have overcome our share of obstacles. We have set our hearts to pursue and welcome the manifest presence of God. We have embraced prophetic words over our lives and partnered with God to see them fulfilled. It has been a challenging and yet rewarding adventure.

As we walked through this journey together, we have learned the empowering quality of declaration and value it highly. This book is a collection of Holy Spirit-inspired declarations that became expressions of our heart and rallying cries along the way. Each one of these declarations came at critical moments in our journey and helped to set our direction and resolve.

The declarations are here for your use. Some of these declarations have found their way into churches in the United States and England and have been translated into Spanish, Swedish, and Romanian. I am thankful they are finding resonance in the hearts of believers, and my prayer is that they will resonate with you as well.

There are declarations in this book that are particularly suited for corporate expression. You are welcome to use them as they are, or you can allow them to inspire your own. Other declarations contained here are more personalized for your inspiration and encouragement. However you choose to live with them, it is my deep desire that *Declarations That Empower Us* will lead you into your own adventure with God as you come into agreement with His purposes for your life—and your world —through the power of declaration.

At the conclusion of each chapter, I have included a page for you to write your own declarations. Giving language to your heart's resolve, crafted in your own words, will help make the declarations personal to your journey.

One warning: declarations can be dangerous to life as you presently know it. Please do not use with caution, but with intentionality.

"There is something
great in you waiting for
you to speak to it."

—Bishop Joseph Garlington

THE
POWER OF
DECLARATION

Death and life are in the power of the tongue.
(Proverbs 18:21, NIV)

Declarations are an indispensable part of life in the kingdom of God. When Jesus taught us, "Your kingdom come, your will be done on earth as it is in heaven,"[1] it was more than an instruction of how to make a prayer request to our Heavenly Father. It was a directive of how to voice a declaration in agreement with the will of the Father.

Everything in the Kingdom begins with a declaration. This is evident from the first declaration by God recorded in Genesis, "Let there be light..." to "Amen! Let it be so!" found in the very

---

[1] Matthew 6:10, NIV.

last chapter of the book of Revelation.

Declarations activate desire, define purpose, and cement intention. They are often the spark that sets things into motion. Bishop Joseph Garlington states:

> *There is something great in you waiting for you to speak to it.*

A couple years before coming to lead the church in Vacaville, California, I was asked to speak at a men's meeting at what is now called The Mission. Late in the afternoon, on the day of the meeting, I spent some time walking around inside of the sanctuary, quietly praying. As I approached the platform and placed my foot on the first step, the following declaration came out of my mouth: "I was made for this."

It shocked me. It did not make sense as I tried to reason it. At the time, I was content pastoring a church in another town and anticipating a long tenure of fruitful ministry. I was not looking for a change in assignment, let alone a change in location. Little did I know that there was something inside of me just waiting for me to speak it out. As I did, that declaration opened my heart to the invitation that would come a couple of years later.

Declarations empower forward motion, reveal intent, and set the mark for future action. At times they draw a line in the sand, steeling our resolve. One of the greatest documents in the history of the United States begins with this statement:

> *When in the Course of human events, it becomes necessary for one people to dissolve the political bands which have connected them with another, and to assume among the powers of the earth, the separate and equal station to which the Laws of Nature and of Nature's God entitle them,*

a decent respect to the opinions of mankind requires that they should declare the causes which impel them to the separation. We hold these truths to be self-evident, that all men are created equal, that they are endowed by their Creator with certain unalienable Rights, that among these are Life, Liberty and the pursuit of happiness.

The document concludes with this declaration:

We, therefore, the Representatives of the United States of America...solemnly publish and declare, that these United Colonies are, and of Right ought to be Free and Independent States; that they are Absolved from all Allegiance to the British Crown, and that all political connection between them and the State of Great Britain, is and ought to be totally dissolved....And for the support of this Declaration, with a firm reliance on the protection of divine Providence, we mutually pledge to each other our Lives, our Fortunes and our sacred honor.

The Declaration of Independence sealed the direction of a people, became the basis of their core values, and led to the establishment of a new nation unlike any other.

It may be surprising to realize that throughout our day, we are actually making declarations in what we say and how we live. Though they may not establish nations, they do have influence in our world. Simple statements, voiced or thought, like "I can't" or "I will" are declarations that carry seeds which will reproduce according to their DNA. A negative declaration will produce negative fruit, and a positive declaration will produce positive fruit.

Declarations have the power to give birth to liberty or to slavery. Solomon was correct when he wrote:

> *Death and life are in the power of the tongue.* (Proverbs 18:21, NIV)

Joshua's declaration, "As for me and my house we will serve the Lord,"[2] moved a nation to choose to walk with God. Job's resolve, "Though He slay me, yet will I trust Him..."[3] sustained him until all that he had lost was fully restored. David's words, "The LORD is my shepherd; I shall not want,"[4] still stand today as a declaration of confidence and comfort for countless millions. When Jesus cried out, "It is finished!"[5] His words were more than the last gasp of a dying man. In that moment, Jesus made the ultimate declaration of the completed work of the cross.

When we make a declaration, we come into agreement with one of two kingdoms: the kingdom of God or the kingdom of darkness. Declarations that are made with faith and in agreement with the Word of God will receive a resounding "Amen!" from Heaven, releasing its full resources and the influence of His kingdom. We actually invite Heaven into our circumstances by the words we speak in faith and the declarations we make.

Declarations begin in the heart. They are the language of the heart's resolves. Resolutions are the issues we have settled in our heart that become platforms from which we operate. They are the bottom lines of our lives. They sustain us in times of trouble and become our default. They hold us to the course when there are few road signs to follow. These hearts resolves make us what we are, and thereby govern our actions and decisions and form the basis for our declarations.

---

2   Joshua 6:15.
3   Job 13:15.
4   Psalm 23:1.
5   John 19:30.

The resolves that produce life come out of fresh revelations of the character and nature of God. They are not the result of our experiences—except where the Father has used those experiences to show us His character. Job's declaration, "Though He slay me, yet I will serve Him,"[6] came out of a revelation of God's majesty and sovereignty, leading him to resolve in his heart that dying with God was better than living without Him. Mary's exclamation, "May it be to me as you have said...,"[7] did not come because she understood the circumstances, but rather, because she had a revelation of God's faithfulness. That revelation settled the issues that had troubled her.

Let me conclude with a personal illustration. On the day that our thirty-one-year-old daughter, Amy, died suddenly in her mother's arms, our world was shattered. The grief was overwhelming, and the sense of loss was devastating. Our hearts physically ached, and it was difficult to even breathe. We walked away from the hospital that day knowing two realities: our daughter was gone, and God was good. The one came from the facts of our present circumstance; the other came through our history with God and by revelation of the Holy Spirit.

Out of that revelation of God's goodness, we began to express our heart resolutions even as we approached our car in the hospital parking lot. I can remember grabbing the handle of the car door and hearing Deborah say through her tears, "I will not live sad, and I will not live mad." That declared resolve became the seed to several other resolutions that became cemented in our hearts over the following months. Those resolutions invited the resources of Heaven into our lives, and to this day, we still hear the echo of Heaven's "Amen."

---

[6] Job 13:15.
[7] Luke 1:38, NIV.

"God is Good" Declarations

Here are some of the resolutions which, during our time of grief, became our declarations, which then become our reality.

WE DECLARE that God is good. Therefore...

We will not sacrifice our destiny or our life message on the altar of our grief.

WE DECLARE that God is good. Therefore...

We will not exchange the joy of the Father for a life of anger, bitterness, or sadness.

WE DECLARE that God is good. Therefore...

Our life message will never be held hostage to our loss.

WE DECLARE that God is good. Therefore...

- The legacy that comes out of this experience will be that our latter years were greater than our former.
- At the place of our deepest loss we choose to become better people.

WE DECLARE that God is good. Therefore...

- We will turn every place of sorrow into a spring of refreshing.
- In every disappointment, we will raise the volume of our worship.
- In the face of every opposition, we will tune our harps and sing the song of the Lord.

My Declaration

Craft your own "God is good..." heart resolutions in this season of your life that lead you to make "Therefore..." declarations.

I believe Jesus is
everything He said He is,
the Father is everything
Jesus said He is,
and the Holy Spirit is
everything Jesus said He is.

Therefore, I believe that
I am everything
Jesus says I am.

Believe

"I believed; therefore I have spoken." Since we have that same spirit of faith, we also believe and therefore speak. (II Corinthians 4:13, NIV)

was flying at about 38,000 feet on my way back from Australia and had 14 hours to kill. The movies did not interest me, and I had already finished the book I had taken on board to keep me occupied. With so many hours of travel yet ahead of me, I decided to just think.

My thoughts led me to ponder the things we "believers" really believe. The more I explored that topic, the more I became convinced that we believers must be certifiably crazy. Consider with me some of the things we believe but do not really think much about:

29

- We believe we hear the voice of an invisible Being, and we make life choices according to what that voice says.

- We study words written in a Book authored by men and believe they are from God—you know, the One who created the universe.

- We also believe that He loves us unconditionally!

- We put our hope in a Man once crucified and believe that He rose from the dead and is living still today!

- We ask forgiveness and actually believe we receive it from that Man.

- Crazier yet, we believe that this Man lives inside us and empowers us to be like Him.

And it does not stop there:

- We also believe that, although every person alive will one day die, we will live beyond death and spend eternity with that crucified Man.

This kind of thinking is dangerous. It can lead us down a slippery slope into believing the illogical logical, the invisible visible, and the non-sensible sensible. If we are not careful, we will become more confident in the impossible than we are in the possible. This could lead to giving more credence to the incredible than the credible. The facts may lose weight to the Truth.

We have already found ourselves refusing to ridicule the ridiculous. We perform prophetic acts and believe that they are doorways into destiny. We make declarations believing they will cause something to happen in us and around us. We knock on closed doors and expect them to open; we ask for the impossible and expect it to come; we command cancer to leave a person's body and believe it will happen—immediately.

Can you believe this?

We stand in the face of overwhelming circumstances and boldly declare the opposite. We live in a collapsing economy yet confess that we live in the economy of something called "the kingdom of God." We seek what cannot be found; we look for what cannot be seen; we listen for a sound not audible to the human ear.

How foolish can we be? Is this all just the creation of a delusional mind? It is so absolutely unbelievable!

Yet, I believe it—all of it.

In the movie, *Elizabeth, the Golden Years,* Queen Elizabeth is having a discussion with her primary consultant, Sir Francis Walsingham, regarding a need for her to make a suitable marriage arrangement. Upon his suggestion of possible suitors, Elizabeth rather offhandedly suggests a couple of improbable ones and receives a measured response from Sir Francis: "I confine myself to the possible."

Elizabeth quickly retorts: "I find the impossible far more interesting."

Well, so do I.

I am not going to take time in this chapter—or this book—to explain why I believe what I believe; but rather, I would like to delineate a little more of what I, as a believer, believe.

This list is not exhaustive by any means. After all, I only had 14 hours on the airplane trip home.

"I Believe..." Declarations

I BELIEVE...

- God is majestically good.

- He is the only true God.

- He is love.

- He is a transformer—He transforms everything that He touches into ultimate worth.

- He is really smart.

- He is trustworthy.

- He is the Three-in-One: He is Father, Son, and Holy Spirit.

- He has prepared a place for me for all of eternity.

While on the subject of "me":

I BELIEVE...

- I am loved and lovable.

- I am God's son.

- I am heir to His fortune; I have an inheritance.

- I am eternally alive; there is life after death.

- I am possessed by Him, and He talks to me.

- I am supernatural.

- I am transformed, being transformed, and transformational.

- I am anointed.

- I am complete in Him.

- I am priceless—of ultimate worth.

- I have an eternal home.

- My hope is sure, my life is secure, and my faith will endure.

- I am His favorite—my picture is on His refrigerator door.

- I am destined to be like Him.

- I inspire His creativity.

- I am holy and righteous.

- I am not a sinner saved by grace; I am a saint.

- I am a prince in my Father's kingdom.

Now that you mention "the kingdom of God":

I also BELIEVE...

- His kingdom is eternal.

- His kingdom is full of joy, peace, and righteousness.

- His kingdom is my true home, now and forever.

- His kingdom is within me, and I am a dispenser of that kingdom.

- His kingdom overpowers the kingdom of darkness.

    In fact, I believe that the kingdoms of this world will be the kingdoms of our God and King.

Just a few more "things" I believe are true to all those who believe:

I BELIEVE...

- All things are possible to him who believes.

- Nothing can separate me from His love.

- All things work together for good to those who love God and are called according to His purpose.

- The Father has put all things under the authority of the Son.

- The things that are seen are temporary, and the things that are unseen are eternal.

- Things invisible are more real than things visible.

  The thing is, I believe!

I BELIEVE that...

- Jesus is the Son of God, born of a virgin.

- He did die for my sins.

- On the third day He rose from the dead.

- Because I believe, I receive the benefit of His death and resurrection—eternal life.

This leads me to believe that:

- My declarations rooted in the Word of the Lord overturn atmospheres and bring into being that which is not.

- When I pray, "Let Your kingdom come..." it comes; when I pray, "Let Your will be done on earth as it is in Heaven...," His will is imposed upon my circumstance.

- My prophetic promises are more than wishful thinking; they are actual doorways into a great destiny.

- I have access to unrestricted possibilities, supernatural

encounters, abundant and consistent refreshing, and an inheritance that cannot be depleted or taken away.

Simply put:

I believe Jesus is everything He said He is, that the Father is everything Jesus said He is, that the Holy Spirit is everything Jesus said He is.

Therefore, I believe that I am everything Jesus says I am.

I BELIEVE!

My Declaration

Craft your own "I believe..." declarations that reflect what you know to be true about who God is, who you are in Christ, the kingdom of God, etc.

_____

_____

_____

_____

_____

_____

_____

_____

_____

_____

_____

_____

_____

It is not the
time to
wait and see,
but to
taste and see.

Jubilee

The Spirit of the Lord GOD is upon Me, because He has anointed Me...to proclaim the acceptable year of the LORD. (Isaiah 61:1, 2)

One of the fondest memories of my childhood is playing the game of hide-and-seek with my many cousins on my grandmother's small farm. As I recollect, it always took place in the warm, summer season of California and usually started around dusk, making the hiding easier and the finding more difficult.

In this computer age of digital games, hide-and-seek may be a lost enjoyment, so let me take a moment to explain how it is played. Hide-and-seek is a game where the one person designated "it" closes their eyes and counts to a predetermined number. While this person is counting, the other players, or "hiders," run and find a hiding place that they hope will keep them from being found. When "it" finishes counting, he (or she) seeks to find one of the hiders. When a hider is found, that person becomes the new "it" and all the other hiders are notified to come out of their hiding places and return back to home base without the risk of becoming the new "it." Being able to come home "free" is the objective of the game.

In order to let the people hiding know that someone has been found and that they are safe to return to base, the person designated "it" yells out the phrase, "Ollie, Ollie oxen free." Or, at least, that is the way we said it. I never really knew what "Ollie, Ollie oxen free" meant, but I was always excited to hear it, knowing that I was free to return to home base. Only later did I discover that "Ollie, Ollie oxen free" is most likely a distortion of an old English phrase, "All ye, all ye, outs in free."

In the early days of Jesus' ministry, it was His custom to go into the local synagogue on the Sabbath. On this particular day, He was invited by the religious leaders to read from the book of Isaiah. The scheduled reading of prophets that week happened to be the passage from chapter 61, the first two verses.

Jesus walked to the front of the synagogue, unrolled the scroll, and read the ancient Isaiah text aloud. All eyes were riveted upon Him. The account from Luke records what happened:

> *The Spirit of the Lord is upon Me, because He has anointed Me to preach the gospel to the poor;*

He has sent Me to heal the brokenhearted, to proclaim liberty to the captives and recovery of sight to the blind, to set at liberty those who are oppressed; to proclaim the acceptable year of the Lord. (4:18,19)

When Jesus finished reading, He rolled up the scroll, sat down, and made a declaration that astounded His audience:

Today, this Scripture is fulfilled in your hearing. (v. 22)

Jesus was clearly identifying Himself to be the "anointed" one referred to in that particular section of Scripture. With this declaration, He announced that from that day forward, the "acceptable year of the Lord" (a reference to the biblical Jubilee year) had commenced. Jesus was declaring to all those in hiding: "All ye, all ye, outs in free!"

The Year of Jubilee referred to the 50th year in Jewish law in which all property that had been sold out of the family estate was to be restored back to its original owner. Also, any Israelite who had sold himself as an indentured bondservant was to be set free.

You can imagine the benefits of such a provision. Inheritances that would otherwise be lost forever were reinstated for the coming generations; bondservants were released to go home, returning the integrity of the family; freedom from slavery restored personal liberties; returned property opened the door for provision and prosperity. Everything shifted in the Jubilee year.

When Jesus declared the Year of Jubilee on that Sabbath morning, He was heralding a new age—an eternal sabbatical—foreshadowed in the law and now a present reality through the work of the cross. Jesus became "it" so that all we "outs" could return home free. He was not making a suggestion, but rather, an eternal heavenly decree authorized by the Father.

The Mission community was the very first to corporately declare the declarations in this chapter after receiving a specific word from the Lord that the year 2012 was highlighted as a Year of Jubilee. We are confident that the Lord is awakening us to embrace the Year of Jubilee as a lifestyle. Since Jesus established our Jubilee over 2,000 years ago, and it has no expiration date, we have unrestricted liberty to continually enjoy its freedoms.

As we have explored God's full intent of Jubilee, we recognize it as a lifetime of reclaiming lost territory, restoring personal freedom, eliminating debt, and even an opportunity to be agents of Jubilee for others.

As you pronounce these declarations, I encourage you to personalize them. Believe them for yourself, your family, and your community.

Jesus said:

> *Did I not say that if you would believe you would see the glory of God?* (John 11:40, NIV)

Don't settle for anything less than experiencing the full measure of Jubilee. This is not the time to wait and see, but to taste and see.

Train your eyes to focus on what God has done and is presently doing, and live with an expectation of what He is yet to do. Behold His glory, and you will be transformed from glory to glory.[8]

---

[8] 2 Corinthians 3:18, NIV.

"Jubilee" Declarations

WE DECLARE this a...

Year of Jubilee.

WE DECLARE this is a...

Year of Unprecedented Opportunity:

- Doors wide open

- Treasure chests unlocked, and

- Fresh divine adventures awaiting us.

WE DECLARE this is a...

Year of Unparalleled Increase:

- Increased revelation

- Increased community

- Increased prosperity, and

- Increased God-encounters.

WE DECLARE this is a...

Year of Unequaled Redemption:

- What has been lost will be recovered

- What has been stolen will be restored with interest, and

- What has been abandoned will be reclaimed.

WE DECLARE that...

In this year, our past failures and wasted opportunities will become stepping-stones into new levels, unexplored territories, and incomparable victories.

WE DECLARE that...

- We are letting go of what was

- Embracing what now is, and

- Reaching with anticipation and expectancy for what will be.

WE DECLARE that...

We now live in the "acceptable year of our Lord"—a lifetime of His commanded blessing, His favor, and our Jubilee.

My Declaration

Craft your own declaration of a lifestyle of Jubilee.

We are a company of dreamers, believers, and friends, and we will not settle for anything less than the manifest presence of Jesus.

3
Community

*I, therefore, the prisoner of the Lord, beseech you
to walk worthy of the calling with which you were
called.* (Ephesians 4:1)

Every local community of believers has a distinct—if not
unique—call and place in the Kingdom. Discovering their
call—their life message—is essential for that community
to be effective in their realm of influence. Defining a church's
specific identity and giving it language empowers its impact and
authority.

Coming to a place of definition is not always easy and cannot
be done in an afternoon think-tank meeting. That which is life-
giving must come by revelation.

At our church, The Mission, we went through several years of having our previous structure and value system dismantled. What we had been was being taken apart, and what we were to become had not yet come into focus. Though this transition was essential, it was a difficult time of disorientation.

One day during this period, my eldest son, Jeremy, was putting a new muffler on his motorcycle in our garage. My wife, Deborah, was curious and inquired about it.

"By adding the muffler," she asked, "are you fixing a problem or will it make the motorcycle run better?"

"No," Jeremy answered. "It won't run any faster and there is no problem with the bike. It'll just make it sound better."

At this, Deborah was convinced that what he was doing was a waste of time and money. But, having raised two boys, she knew better than to pursue the matter with any more questioning.

A few days later, Deborah had a dream. In the dream, she saw a field strewn with a variety of mechanical parts. She could tell they were parts from a lawnmower. The Lord told her that we had been that lawnmower—something used to keep things neat and in order. What He was transitioning us into, instead, was an earthmoving machine that could take down mountains and make roads. However, in order to do that, He had to dismantle what was, so we would not simply add something to the lawnmower to make it sound better, run faster, and cut cleaner.

We realized that we had to be willing to allow the Lord to dismantle us personally and our structure and values corporately; otherwise, left up to us, we would simply be making improvements to the lawnmower.

Thankfully, this process did not last forever.

One of the revelations that helped to bring some definition to our call and life message was a list of decisions that came to me one day as a download from the Holy Spirit. We have called them "Decisions that Define Us." When I spoke these declarative decisions over the church at the graduation ceremony of our supernatural training school, with one heart we all agreed, "This is who we are."

These decisions started us on a journey of discovering and defining the community we were becoming. They continue to give language to our pursuit as a company of people seeking first His kingdom. They have even traveled around the world and given inspiration and encouragement to many local church communities. They are the foundation of my book, *Decisions That Define Us*,[9] and can also be found in my second book, *The Power of Your Life Message*.[10]

The declarations presented in this chapter were first expressed in a corporate gathering at The Mission. It was a time of restating the commitment to our call as a company of people fully pursuing the kingdom of God. They include some of the "Decisions that Define Us" restated as declarations. Since we are engaged in an ongoing journey, I also include other declarations here that have come from walking with our community in this great adventure.

---

[9] Crone, David. *Decisions That Define Us*, Mark 16:15 International. Book available online at: imissionchurch.com.
[10] Crone, David. *The Power of Your Life Message*, Mark 16:15 International. Book available online at: imissionchurch.com.

"Community" Declarations

WE DECLARE...

That we have an inheritance that provides spiritual territory for those of this community and others who will come to enjoy its freedom.

WE DECLARE...

That this is a house of increase, where people will come from every direction to have fresh encounters with God.

WE DECLARE...

That this is a house where no one is safe from a blessing.

WE DECLARE...

That we are a people and a place of His abiding presence.

WE DECLARE...

That we are a people and a place of God's indulgence.

WE DECLARE...

That we are a people and a place where His Gospel is demonstrated, not just taught.

WE DECLARE...

That we are a company of worshipers hosting the manifest presence of God.

WE DECLARE...

That we are those who believe reading about the book

of Acts without living the book of Acts is unthinkable.

WE DECLARE...

That we are Holy Spirit-filled, Holy Spirit-led, and Holy Spirit-empowered—anything less does not work for us.

WE DECLARE...

That we are the ones telling the stories of God's power, not just hearing about them.

WE DECLARE...

That we will live saved and supernatural.

WE DECLARE that we are...

- A battle ship not a cruise ship,
- An army not an audience,
- Special Forces not spectators,
- Missionaries not club members.

WE DECLARE...

That both pioneers and settlers are valuable, but we refuse to be squatters.

WE DECLARE that we are...

- Infectious instead of innocuous,
- Contagious instead of quarantined,
- Deadly instead of benign.

WE DECLARE...

That we are radical lovers and outrageous givers.

WE DECLARE...

That we are a mission station, not a museum.

WE DECLARE...

That we will not be satisfied until our world cries out, "Those who have turned the world upside down have come here too."[11]

WE DECLARE...

That we are a company of dreamers, believers, and friends, and we will not settle for anything less than the manifest presence of Jesus, an experiential relationship with Holy Spirit, and a daily encounter with Father God.

---

[11] Acts 17:6.

My Declaration

Craft your own declaration that reflects God's heart to advance His kingdom through you and your community of believers.

_____

_____

_____

_____

_____

_____

_____

_____

_____

_____

_____

_____

_____

Since we have the
Word of the Lord and
we believe it,
we are on our way to
becoming a great company—
as we proclaim it.

4
Enough

The Lord gave the word; great was the company of those who proclaimed it. (Psalm 68:11)

There is a great picture in Scripture of what happens when God stands up in our difficult situations and declares, "Enough!"

Let God arise, let His enemies be scattered; let those also who hate Him flee before Him.

As smoke is driven away, so drive them away; as wax melts before the fire, so let the wicked perish at the presence of God. But let the righteous be glad; let them rejoice before God; yes, let them rejoice exceedingly. (Psalm 68:1-3)

Atmospheres shift at the sound of His voice. Circumstances bow at His name so that disabilities are healed, diseases are defeated, and wasted lives become useful. Mercy prevails, justice is accomplished, and grace wins the day.

The premise of the following declarations is that God has already stood up and said, "Enough!" Jesus was not making light conversation when He publicly announced that He came to destroy the works of the enemy. He came to Earth at the invitation of the Father and cried out with a loud voice from the cross, "Enough!" to the power and consequence of sin; He emphatically declared, "Enough!" to the power of disease and illness by taking the stripes on His back; He shouted in triumph, "Enough!" to the power of death at His resurrection.

Could it be that all God is waiting for, is for us to stand up in the situation we presently find ourselves and make our own personal declarations in agreement with His? I believe so. Though there are always timing and obedience issues with God, I have a sense there are many breakthroughs that have already been agreed to by Him, but they are left on the table simply because we do not take up our position and declare aloud with Him, "Enough!"

Further on in Psalm 68, David writes:

The Lord gave the word; great was the company of those who proclaimed it. (v. 11)

I would like to suggest that since we have the Word of the Lord and we believe it, we are on our way to becoming a great company—as we proclaim it.

The story of building the 37,000-square-foot sanctuary of The Mission is a testimony of miraculous provision. Prior to its completion, we had a history of deep debt and abandoned projects. Yet, we were convinced that God had instructed us to build it and to build it debt free. This meant that we could only continue construction as long as the money was in the bank and available for use.

There came a point in the construction that we knew we did not have enough funds to complete the project. We were 1.2 million dollars short. The exterior was complete while stacks of drywall filled the massive interior waiting to be installed. It would be just a matter of days before we would have to call a halt to construction.

I can still remember the feeling of frustration on Monday morning as I anticipated announcing to the congregation that we were unable to continue the construction. While my frustration level increased all that day and into the evening, a determination was also beginning to rise in my spirit. My heart reviewed God's leading thus far: This building project was God's idea, and His promise to us was that its testimony and miraculous provision would be part of our legacy.

As my spirit was strengthened, I knew it was time to say, "Enough!" to lack and come into agreement with God's Word to us about His sanctuary.

"Deb, I'm going to the church to pray," I called out to my wife. "Do you want to come with me?" She did, and we also invited my eldest son, Jeremy, to accompany us. The three of us entered the darkened shell that was to become our sanctuary, flashlights in hand, with a firm determination to declare breakthrough into the atmosphere.

Jeremy and Deborah climbed onto two separate piles of sheetrock, and I took the stairs up to what was to become the video suite from where I could overlook the interior of the building. Together, perched at three points in the future sanctuary, we began to declare the Scriptures and the prophetic promises that God had given us over the previous months. We did this until we felt a release. After about fifteen minutes or so, we climbed down from our perches and returned home, highly anticipating God's response.

The next day, I had an appointment to give a tour of the construction progress to a man who had already been very generous to the project. At one point in the conversation, I shared with him that we were about to stop construction.

"We have an immediate need to raise the remainder of the money before we continue building," I explained.

My friend leaned forward, the pleasure on his face clearly evident, and said, "Well, I had already set aside an additional $800,000 for this project, just in case you might need it."

I was astonished as I stood there listening to his response. In that moment, my mind was in a whirlwind of thoughts and emotions as I recalled the prophetic declarations we had made just the day before in the unfinished sanctuary, fully expecting breakthrough.

He continued, "I will have the funds transferred to the account tomorrow."

A few weeks later, during our Sunday morning service, the remaining $400,000 needed to complete the project was raised. There it was: the testimony of God's miraculous provision. God had said, "Enough!" to our lack, we came into agreement, and the sanctuary was completed.

The following declarations fall into three distinct arenas of life: health, relationships, and finances. I encourage you to stand in agreement with God and be expectant for breakthrough.

"Enough!" Declarations

Health

These declarations over your health are powerful tools to come into agreement with God's Word regarding healing. Just as powerful are the tools of proper sleep, healthy eating, and regular exercise. Implementing a healthy lifestyle ensures that your body will stay in agreement with the way God created it to function normally and also to maintain the healing you receive.

WE DECLARE...

That our bodies are the temple of the Holy Spirit and that God is our healer.

WE DECLARE...

That the same Spirit who raised Jesus from the dead lives in us and gives life to our mortal bodies.

WE DECLARE...

That complete health is the nature of the kingdom of God.

WE DECLARE...

That the stripes on Jesus' back are for our healing and that physical health is our Father's will.

Therefore:

WE SAY, "Enough!"

To illness, disease, and injury.

WE SAY, "Enough!"

To cancer of every kind, immunodeficiency disease, respiratory illnesses, and diabetes.

WE SAY, "Enough!"

To pulmonary disease, brain disorders, and nervous conditions.

WE SAY, "Enough!"

To heart disease, heart attacks, and strokes.

WE DECLARE...

That we have had "Enough!" and we take hold of the work of the cross and receive our physical health, vitality, and strength.

Relationships

Relationships require maintenance and investment. Bruised and broken relationships require humility and wisdom. As you make these declarations over your relationships, listen to the Holy Spirit for needed adjustments in your own attitudes and actions, along with any strategies for restoration.

Remember, every one of our choices comes out of one of two emotions—love or fear. Choose well.

WE DECLARE...

That the Holy Spirit is our peacemaker and the reconciler of broken and bruised relationships.

WE DECLARE...

That we have been given the ministry of reconciliation as children of God.

Therefore:

WE SAY, "Enough!"

To shattered, damaged, and estranged relationships.

WE SAY, "Enough!"

To unfaithfulness, irreconcilable differences, and divorce.

WE SAY, "Enough!"

To contention and hostility.

WE SAY, "Enough!"

To the enemy's plans to separate, disconnect, and destroy family relationships.

WE SAY, "Enough!"

To the demonic spirits of hostility, rejection, contention, control, and manipulation; and we release the Spirit of love, generosity, thanksgiving, and grace.

WE DECLARE...

The return of the prodigal and the recovery of the lost.

WE DECLARE...

The return of children to parents and parents to children.

WE DECLARE...

The godly resolution of conflict and the completion of healthy relational agreements.

WE SAY, "Enough!"

To the kingdom of darkness and declare the kingdom of

righteousness, peace, and joy as the ruling kingdom in every one of our relationships.

Finances

Scripture is filled with expressions of the Father's heart that we be prosperous. Therefore, we can make these declarations with great confidence. Scripture is also replete with wisdom and instruction regarding the stewardship of our resources. It is futile to agree with the Father's heart to bless on the one hand, yet ignore our responsibility to steward on the other.

As you proclaim the following declarations, make your resolve to discover and follow the strategies of stewardship that will position you for healthy financial living.

WE DECLARE...

That God is our financial source; we declare that His resource is unlimited and not tied to this world's economy.

WE DECLARE...

That the day of loss is over, and the day of increase has begun.

WE SAY, "Enough!"

- To leanness and barrenness

- "Enough!" to joblessness and foreclosures

WE SAY, "Enough!"

- To lost wages and decreased benefits

- "Enough!" to business closures, bank failures, and bankruptcies

WE DECLARE...

That we are in agreement with God's "Enough!" and that our God is more than enough.

Therefore:

WE DECLARE...

- Jobs and more jobs
- Raises and bonuses
- Increased benefits
- Sales and commissions
- Settlements, estates, and inheritances

WE DECLARE...

- Rebates and returns
- Checks in the mail
- Gifts and surprises
- Found money
- Debts paid off
- Bills decreasing, and
- Blessings increasing

WE SAY, "Enough!"

To limited supply, and we declare our allegiance "to Him who is able to do exceedingly abundantly above all that we ask or think..."[12]

---

[12] Ephesians 3:20.

My Declaration

Craft your personal declaration that reflects God's desire to bless you with healing and health, good relationships, and financial prosperity.

Where we might settle
for a canteen of refreshing,
hope, and blessing,
God offers rivers, springs,
and fountains.

5 More than Enough

Now to Him who is able to do exceedingly abundantly, above all that we ask or think, according to the power that works in us. (Ephesians 3:20, NIV)

I was standing with friends of mine in the emergency waiting room of our local hospital on a sunny afternoon. From across the room, a man with a noticeably damaged right shoulder approached me and asked if I would please step outside with him for a moment. As the door closed behind us, the man turned to me and asked, "Is it true you are a pastor?" He had obviously heard one of my colleagues address me.

"Yes," I confirmed. "I am one of the pastoral leaders at a church nearby."

Looking a bit relieved at my response, the man began to share some of his life story and expressed his desire to "make things right with God." It gave me great pleasure to lead him into a relationship with Jesus Christ right there, and then to watch as God does what He does best—transform.

After he regained an emotional equilibrium, he thanked me and then turned to walk back into the waiting room.

"Wait a minute..." I called after him. "Can you tell me what the problem is with your shoulder?" It was evident that he was in a lot of pain.

"I fell off my motorcycle," he explained.

"Let me pray for you again!" I offered. "The same God who just forgave you and welcomed you as His son is also a healer!"

*This is going to be great...*I thought, *saved and healed—all in the same day!* The man's response, however, really surprised me.

"Oh, that's okay. I got what I needed. I don't want to bother Him." With that he turned and walked back into the hospital. It was as if this man believed that with God you have to choose A, B, or C, but you certainly can't have it all.

Sadly, I have observed this same mindset among many believers. Yet, the Prophet Isaiah paints a picture that is vastly different from such a concept of God.

> *The poor and needy search for water, but there is none; their tongues are parched with thirst. But I the LORD will answer them;*

> *I, the God of Israel, will not forsake them. I will make rivers flow on barren heights, and springs within the valleys. I will turn the desert into pools of water, and the parched ground into springs.*

I will put in the desert the cedar and the acacia, the myrtle and the olive. I will set pines in the wasteland, the fir and the cypress together so that people may see and know, may consider and understand, that the hand of the LORD has done this, that the Holy One of Israel has created it. (41:17-20, NIV)

In this section of Scripture, Isaiah describes thirsty people and thirsty places and then gives God's answer to each. In so doing, the prophet presents a God who is more than enough for all we need.

As you read this passage, you will see that, to those whose lofty dreams have run out of provision, God offers rivers in their desolate heights. To those living in discouragement and despair, He delivers fountains of refreshing to their valley. To those who cannot see the forest for the trees, God creates a pool in their wilderness. To those who are emotionally, physically, and mentally weary, He releases springs of life-giving water to their dry land.

These are not the expressions of a stingy or limited God. Where we might settle for a canteen of refreshing, hope, and blessing, He offers these in rivers, springs, and fountains. God even makes our pools the size of our wilderness! His provision not only meets the need, it transforms the landscape.

My wife, Deborah, is an accomplished artist and has an open invitation to paint during the conferences held at Bethel Church in Redding, California. On one such occasion, she experienced a revelation of just how more-than-enough God really is.

The night before she was to paint during the worship service of the Leaders Advance conference, she had a significant dream. In the dream, a man came up to her and offered to buy a small painting that Deborah had on the platform where she was painting. He said to her, "That painting is mine."

Deborah felt an agreement in her spirit that the painting was indeed to be given to this particular man and his wife as a gift. As she was about to tell him this, the man said to her, "But I will not pay the listed price for your painting."

He went on to tell her, "I will not pay $200 for that painting. I'm going to pay $250 instead."

Then, almost without hesitation he continued, "No, I won't pay $250 for that painting...I'll pay $400 for it."

All the while Deborah attempted unsuccessfully to explain her intentions to give the painting to them both as a gift.

Then, the dream ended.

The next evening, at the end of the service, the very man Deborah had seen in her dream came directly to her art display booth. Then, it just seemed as if he picked up where her dream had left off the night before.

"That painting is mine," he declared in no uncertain terms, "but I will not pay what you are asking; I will pay $400 for the painting!"

Deborah stood there dumbfounded trying to express to him that she simply wanted to give the painting to him as a gift. But, on and on he continued—as in the dream—increasing the price of his previous offer.

He finally ended the price negotiation by stating, "I will pay $1,000 for that painting!" With that final offer, the man pulled out a check he had already made out to Deborah for this exact amount.

"I sensed, from the Lord," the man explained, handing the check to Deborah, "that the number '1,000' had a special significance in your life."

He was absolutely correct. In fact, the Lord had been encouraging Deborah for several weeks to ask Him for the blessings of a thousand generations. She sensed God was granting her permission, and this experience became a vivid confirmation to go ahead and ask with full confidence that the outcome of her request would be abundantly fruitful.

Testimonies such as these are an example of the generosity of God for all we need and the manifestation of His extravagant nature that is always more than enough.

The declarations in this chapter come into agreement with the Scriptures that portray a God Who is more than enough: He is exceedingly, abundantly above all, and His generosity always goes beyond our expectation.

"More than Enough" Declarations

WE DECLARE that...

- We are children of the King.

- As His children we are qualified for every royal blessing, provision, favor, and inheritance.

WE DECLARE that...

- Our God is generous beyond measure;

- He is enough and more than enough to turn our desolation into a river of abundant provision,

- Our valley into a fountain of life-giving encouragement,

- Our wilderness into a pool of thirst-quenching refreshment; and

- Our dry land into springs of outrageous blessing.

WE DECLARE that...

In Christ are found all the treasures of wisdom and knowledge and that we are in Christ.

Therefore:

We are complete in Him, and in Him, we are more than enough for every challenge, opportunity, and cause.

We come into agreement with the power that works in us to:

- Reach that which is presently out of our reach

- Accomplish that which, in the natural, is impossible

- Be the people He has declared us to be.

WE DEDICATE...

- Our minds to think what God thinks,

- Our mouths to declare what the Spirit of Christ declares, and

- Our lives to reflect that we are children of Jehovah Jireh—the God who is—

More than enough!

My Declaration

Craft your own declaration about how God's generosity towards you as more than enough.

Expressions of delight
help set our focus on
the goodness of God and the privilege
of our relationship with a good and
generous Father.

Delight

Delight yourself in the LORD and he will give you the desires of your heart. (Psalm 37:4, NIV)

One of the keys to living a captivating life is to be captivated by something or someone. David expresses his captivation with God throughout the Psalms, but says it most clearly in Psalm 27 when he writes:

> *One thing I have desired of the LORD, that will I seek: That I may dwell in the house of the LORD all the days of my life, to behold the beauty of the LORD, and to inquire in His temple.* (v. 4, NIV)

According to Strong's Concordance, the Hebrew word used here for "beauty"[13] is "delightfulness, pleasantness; a delightful loveliness." David was captivated by the presence of God and took his pleasure in the delightfulness of the Lord. This, I believe is what it means to "delight yourself in the Lord."

David again expresses the heart of his passion when he cries out:

> *In your presence is fullness of joy; at your right hand are pleasures for evermore.* (Psalm 16:11)

The word "fullness"[14] means "a satisfying abundance of both quality and quantity," and the word "pleasures"[15] can be translated "delights." Adding to that, the word "evermore"[16] speaks of the distance from here to the horizon. When you put all that together, you have the following amplification:

> *In Your presence, God, there is an available abundance of satisfying joy; and with that comes delights* [things that we can take delight in] *that stretch out before us for as far as we can see. These delights are immeasurable because, as we move forward in them, they continue to fill the landscape all the way to the horizon.*

One of my Christmas traditions for several years was to take a few family members shopping on Christmas Eve and let them pick out a present for themselves. Sometimes I would take my grandchildren; other years I would take my daughter

---

[13] *Blueletterbible.org, Strong's Concordance,* Old Testament Hebrew Lexicon, H5278 "beauty", Heb., *noam.*

[14] *Ibid.,* H7648 "fullness", Heb., *soba'.*

[15] *Ibid.,* H5273 "pleasures", Heb., *naimot.*

[16] *Ibid.,* H5331 "evermore", Heb., *netzach.*

and two daughters-in-law. Taking my three girls was always an interesting experience in observation.

As we would enter a jewelry store, I would say to them, "Pick out something you really would like to have. Choose whatever you want." My daughters-in-law, Jennifer and Desiree, would quickly respond in embarrassment and try to convince me that they didn't need or want anything. As I would apply a little pressure to choose something that really appealed to them, they would most often select something of little cost and not something a little more extravagant, as I had hoped. They would simply settle on an item I knew was of little value to them. Though I love my sons' wives as my own daughters, their response left me less than satisfied.

My daughter, Amy, however, had no such hesitation or reticence. She would go about the store with great zeal choosing several things from which to make her selection. Her response to my offer gave me a great amount of pleasure as she allowed me to indulge myself on her. She was delighting in me and in my father's heart to give and to bless her generously.

This is a great picture of what it looks like to delight in the Lord—to give the Father pleasure by partaking of all the delights He has offered us.

Taking delight in the Lord is actively and intentionally living in the favor of God, allowing ourselves the pleasure of His company, and purposefully indulging in all He is and does. David even dares to suggest that the very desires of our heart are released when we delight in the Lord:

> *Delight yourself also in the Lord, and He will give*
> *you the desires of your heart.* (Psalm 37:4)

Delighting ourselves in the Lord authorizes our permission to dream and takes the lid off our possibilities.

Declaring our intention to delight in the Lord is not a religious exercise but, rather, a purposeful directing of our hearts and minds to see and experience His delights in every circumstance of life. Expressions of delight help set our focus on the goodness of God and the privilege of our relationship with a good and generous Father. Speaking them out loud invades and brightens the atmosphere we carry with us throughout the day and prepares us to take hold of the reality of the tremendous abundance He offers us.

I have listed some of my own personal expressions of delight in the following declarations. However, I encourage you to add some of your own. Write them out; meditate on them; set your MP3 player to your favorite music, and declare them out loud.

Start your day captivated by the delightfulness of His presence.

Declaration of Delight

Father,

I delight myself...

In You today.

I delight myself...

- In Your love,
- In Your mercy,
- In Your compassion, and
- In Your faithfulness.

I receive the gifts You have prepared for me, and
I take joy in the pleasure of Your company.

I delight myself...

- In the day You have designed for me,
- In the opportunities You have made available, and
- In the promises You are fulfilling in this day.

I delight myself...

In Your goodness.

I delight myself...

In You.

My Declaration

In your own words, craft a declaration of how you delight in the Lord.

Could it be that the
times of great pressure
are invitations into
times of our greatest
increase?

7
Living Large

You have enlarged me in my distress. (Psalm 4:1, AKJV)

Everyone knows what it is like to live under pressure. We all understand days, weeks, and even years when circumstances press in on us making us feel overwhelmed and crowded into a small space.

It is no secret that the enemy of our lives has come to kill, steal, and destroy, and that one of his goals is to reduce our lives to being controlled by the situations around us. If he can do this, he will cause us to respond to life from a constrained place, thereby limiting our vision, our faith, and our hope.

This mode of living with limitations, however, is not what Jesus died to give us. He came to give us life—a more abundant life. This does not mean that we will not experience pressures, crises, or the pressing circumstances of life, but rather, in the midst of such stressing difficulties, we can live large on the inside and make choices from a spacious place.

"The one who is in you is greater than the one who is in the world,"[17] is more than wishful thinking. It can be a living reality.

David was a king on the run. Though anointed by the Prophet Samuel to be king, he was being chased by Saul and living in caves. He went from being the hero of the battle with Goliath to being a fugitive in hiding. In Psalm 18, David reflects on this particular time in his life, describing the goodness of God through it all, and makes this amazing declaration:

> *You enlarged my path under me, so my feet did not slip.* (v. 36, NKJV)

David was saying: "In this narrow place I walked on a wide path—I lived large in the time of pressure and constraint. The path under my feet was larger than the space around me."

David was living larger than life in limiting circumstances. He expressed a similar thought recorded in Psalm 4:1.

> *You have enlarged me in my distress.* (AKJV)

He knew that though he was being crowded and restricted by circumstances, God had increased him on the inside so that he could live from a wide-open and spacious place.

Could it be that the times of great pressure are invitations into times of our greatest increase?

---

[17]   1 John 4:4, NIV.

Bernard Cornwell, British-born novelist, is one of my favorite historical authors. In his book, *The Pale Horseman*,[18] Cornwell tells the story of Alfred the Great and his dream to unite England under one rule. At one point during this endeavor, King Alfred finds himself and his small army reduced to living in a small patch of marshland while the rest of England has been taken over by the invading Danish forces. Alfred uses this time to build up his troops and prepare for what he knows will be the one battle that will determine the future of England. He is badly outnumbered and under-equipped, but he realizes he can wait no longer.

The narrator of the story is a fictitious hero named Uhtred, a famed swordsman who had made the difference in many previous battles. When King Alfred gave the command to move the troops out to battle, Uhtred comments on the call:

> *Though reason and numbers said we could not win, we dared not lose. So we marched.*[19]

History tells us that they did indeed march, and, in the face of the worst possible circumstances, secured the victory for England.

Deborah and I could never have imagined what it would be like to live life after the death of a child. Then came the day when we no longer had to imagine it as our 31-year-old daughter died suddenly in Deborah's arms. In that moment, we both felt as if our hearts stopped beating.

Living in that reality is beyond description. The pressure to withdraw and abandon life is very real. The attempts of the enemy to shrink our world into a room full of grief and pain were many. During each episode of overwhelming sorrow, we were faced with the choice of narrowing our lives or stepping into the

---

[18] Cornwell, Bernard. *The Pale Horseman*, HarperCollins, 2006.
[19] *Ibid.*

broad place God offered us on the inside. Though circumstances told us we could not win, we marched. Each and every time we took God up on His offer, our internal world expanded, and we were able to live from that broadened place.

Hebrews 10:35-39 has always been for me a call to endurance during exceptionally challenging times. I wrote the passage out in a personal, amplified version based upon my own extensive word study of the text. It follows here:

> *Do not throw away, or lose by default, your free and fearless assurance, which, of its own, is of great benefit. For through your tenacious determination to not give up on what God has promised, you will receive that promise.*
>
> *There is a time delay between the promise and its fulfillment, creating pressure to draw back and give up territory that has been designated for you. It is territory that is your inheritance; it belongs to you, and it is the Father's good pleasure to give it to you. By drawing back, you rob the Father of His pleasure in seeing you possess what is yours.*
>
> *However, that will not happen. We will not cower under the pressure and yield territory that belongs to us because we are those who, in faith, take hold of all that has been given to us, and we are becoming all we have been created to be. We will live large, even in the narrow places.*

The following declarations are based on several passages of Scripture and have come out of our personal journey as well as the corporate journey of those we are privileged to live large with at The Mission.

"Living Large" Declarations

WE DECLARE...

That it is the Father's good pleasure to give us the Kingdom.

WE DECLARE...

That in Christ we are more than enough for every challenge, opportunity, and cause.

WE DECLARE...

- That the One in us is greater than the circumstance around us;

- That His presence on the inside is mightier than the pressure on the outside;

- That the Spirit of the Holy One overwhelms any other one.

Therefore:

We come into agreement with the power that works in us to:

- Live from eternity, not from our circumstances,

- Reap in the season of famine,

- Increase in the time of lack,

- Expand in the time of pressure.

In the narrow places we will:

- Believe greater,

- Walk stronger, and

- Live larger.

Therefore:

WE WILL walk in every storm with a free and fearless assurance, confident that the God who is able to do exceedingly abundantly above all we ask or think is in the storm with us.

My Declaration

Craft a declaration of how you are living large in a spacious place even in a season of difficult circumstances.

We have decided

that it is better to fail while reaching

for the impossible that

God has planned for us

than to succeed settling for less.

Never
the Less

Master, we have toiled all night and caught nothing; nevertheless at Your word I will let down the net. (Luke 5:5)

I t was a moment of decision for Simon Peter.

"Do I tell this carpenter-turned-itinerate-preacher that he doesn't know what he's talking about, dry out my nets and call it a day, or climb back in my boat and do as He says—'Go fish?'"

It had been a long night for Peter, a night of complete futility for a man who made his living by fishing. Nothing, not a single fish had been caught in his net. He was tired and disappointed.

"Just what I need," he must have thought, "a preacher telling me how to run my business..."

Little did Peter realize that his response to Jesus' command would, in reality, determine the rest of his life. In that moment, Peter could not help but remind Jesus of the facts: "We have fished all night and caught nothing."

You and I know what that's like: After we have prayed, fasted, declared, and worshiped, still the circumstance remains unchanged in defiance of the fulfillment of God's promise to us. We have done everything we know to do in order to partner with God for the breakthrough, yet we remain stuck in the same situation. The temptation at this point is to hang up our nets and give up. I think it is safe to say that at times we, too, have reminded God of the futility of our efforts, just as Peter did—"We fished all night and caught nothing."

Peter's next words are recorded as a challenge to us.

Nevertheless, at Your word I will let down the nets.
(NIV)

Responding to Jesus in this way, Peter risked the potential for failure as well as ridicule from his fellow fishermen. Yielding to the instructions of Jesus ignored reasonable fishing wisdom and looked past the obvious facts of a night without reward. But the result of his response not only brought Peter a catch he could not contain, it opened up a future he could never have imagined possible. His surrender to Jesus that morning would take him from futility to destiny.

Now, take a fresh look at Peter's response and see the first word, not as one word, but as three: "never the less." In that moment Peter took Jesus at His word and decided to go for something much greater.

Herein lies our choice: Dare we risk failure, ignore the facts or present circumstance, and at the word of the Lord declare,

"Never the less—always the greater"? It certainly doesn't sound reasonable, does it? But the kingdom of God is not a reasonable kingdom. Asking a seasoned, professional fisherman to let down his nets at the wrong time of the day, in a place where fishing all night caught nothing, is an unreasonable request. Yet Peter chose to not settle for less and, instead, rested his professional career on the word of Jesus.

Never the less—always the greater.

The following declarations establish our hearts to come into agreement with an unreasonable "never-the-less" lifestyle. They are confessions of our faith and conviction that the Word of God is greater than any circumstance. At His Word, we will look past our history, risk failure, and put our lives on the line for "the greater" God has promised.

In the declaration, "The Decisions that Define Us," we made the following choice:

> We have decided that it is better to fail while reaching for the impossible that God has planned for us than to succeed settling for less.

"Never the Less" Declarations

WE DECLARE...

That God's Word is living and powerful.

WE DECLARE...

That what He has spoken will come to pass.

WE DECLARE...

That our circumstances must bow to the truth of God's Word.

Therefore:

FROM THIS MOMENT ON...

When the potential for failure is present, at His word I choose "Never the less—always the greater."

FROM THIS MOMENT ON...

When the fear of man is present, at His Word I choose "Never the less—always the greater."

FROM THIS MOMENT ON...

When the facts oppose His Word, at His Word I choose "Never the less—always the greater."

FROM THIS MOMENT ON...

When the evidence of my history stands in the way of my obedience, at His word, I choose "Never the less—always the greater."

FROM THIS MOMENT ON...

When my faith is weak, at His word, I choose "Never the less—always the greater."

FROM THIS MOMENT ON...

I choose to give thanks for what is and confess the future God's Word has declared for me.

FROM THIS MOMENT ON...

I choose "Never the less—always the greater."

My Declaration

Craft your own declaration that reflects your determination to reach for the impossible and always choose "Never the less—always the greater."

When we accept
the fullness of the work of
the cross
and our adoption as sons,
we become vulnerable
to favor.

Favor

Jesus increased in wisdom and stature and in favor
with God and men. (Luke 2:52, NIV)

I am a visual guy. I need to be able to see something in order to understand it. Unless an image comes to mind, simply hearing a concept does not help me grasp it. God knows this about me and often teaches me about Himself and His kingdom through common experiences that become windows of understanding. This was especially true when He began to teach me about His favor.

One of my first lessons in favor came through what has become routine in my life—air travel. This initial instruction took place several years ago as Deborah and I arrived early one morning at the San Francisco International Airport to catch a flight to Maui, Hawaii.

When we entered the terminal, the lines of people waiting to check-in seemed to be miles long. It was like everyone in California was heading to Maui on the same flight. I hate lines. It's not that I am impatient; it is just that I do not like to wait. Since this was before I had any frequent flyer status with the airlines, we did not have any choice but to take our place reluctantly at the end of the line. It was evident to us that this was going to be a long morning of trudging slowly toward our objective.

After only a few minutes of waiting in line, however, a man dressed in what looked like a porter's uniform came towards us, reached under the rope, grabbed one of our suitcases, and began walking down the terminal. Without any explanation whatsoever, he simply motioned that we were to follow him. This took us by such complete surprise that we stood there for a moment, staring after him, not really sure what to do. Then, we grabbed our remaining suitcases and followed our quickly disappearing luggage.

We hurried to follow after the porter past the long lines waiting to check-in until we finally came to a kiosk at the far end of the terminal. There, a United Airlines agent stood behind the counter, preoccupied on his computer. The porter placed all of our suitcases on the weight scale, asked us for our tickets, and promptly presented these to the agent. Without comment or questioning, the agent processed the tickets, rapidly typing into his terminal, reached down to the printer at his feet and returned with our boarding passes. He then tagged our luggage and tossed them onto the conveyer belt. All the while, Deborah and I stood there puzzled by all of this and tried to make sense of what was happening. This was certainly not normal processing of airline passengers.

The agent then handed us our passes, smiled, and said,

"Have a good flight." As the next people waiting in line moved forward, we looked at the boarding passes and realized that we had been upgraded to premium seats. Favor!

We turned around to tip our porter and thank him, but he was nowhere to be found. We wondered in that moment if God had sent an angel to assist us, but, as we stood in line for security a few moments later, I spotted him and was able to express our appreciation.

Over the years since that first encounter, we have enjoyed similar experiences of God's favor many times. Each of them has been a new lesson on what it is like to walk in the favor of the Lord; every time, I come away with a fresh appreciation for the goodness of God.

Favor is the result of Christ's work on the Earth. Every place Jesus broke through created a doorway for us to walk through. Wherever Jesus took territory, He opened that territory for us to occupy. This is true with many things, and it is certainly true of His favor on us.

Luke records this about Jesus:

> *Jesus increased in wisdom and stature and in favor with God and men.* (2:52, NIV)

His breakthrough in favor gives us permission to apprehend favor for ourselves.

Favor is a continual process, and it should be increasing in our lives as it did in the life of Jesus. In other words, the level of favor you enjoy tomorrow should be greater than the level you enjoy today. Increasing in favor requires more than the passing of time; it requires intentionality on our part. To increase means to advance, to make progress. Though favor is available to all believers, only those who intentionally apprehend it experience and increase in it.

Accepting the lie that we are not worthy of favor is probably the number one limiting factor to experiencing God's favor. Declaring ourselves unworthy keeps us from expecting an increase in favor, and expectation is a key factor to experiencing favor. If you believe yourself unworthy, you will not be looking for favor, you dare not ask for it, and you will not be able to recognize it, even in a clearly obvious situation.

The work of the cross is the basis of our favor, for the cross is what made us worthy. We do not deserve His favor, but it is never about whether we deserve it or not. Favor is, after all, undeserved. Favor is not entitlement but is rooted in the goodness of God from whom every good and perfect gift comes. It is not arrogance but confidence in the One who made us accepted in the Beloved. When we accept the fullness of the work of the cross and our adoption as sons, we become vulnerable to favor.

I have learned that expectation attracts favor; therefore, I have trained myself to be expectant which, in turn, positions me for favor. It is important to test it and put weight on it— like Esther did before the king and as Abraham did when he bargained with God to spare the righteous living in unrighteous cities.

Favor is God signing and cashing the checks that I have written. It is not presumption to write the checks. It is, in a sense, taking my favor for a spin.

Favor is grace demonstrated; grace is an empowerment to live as we ought.

I have also learned that generosity attracts favor. Everything we have been given is to give away. You want to attract favor? Give it away.

Jesus said:

> *Give, and it will be given to you: good measure, pressed down, shaken together, and running over will be put into your bosom....* (Luke 6:38)

That's favor. Jesus also said:

Do not be deceived, God is not mocked, whatever a man sows, that he will also reap. (Galatians 6:7, NIV)

That's not a threat; it's a promise! Favor sown reaps favor. Bringing others into your favor will not only increase your favor, it is a lot of fun!

A few years ago, a couple from The Mission accompanied Deborah and me on a ministry trip to Italy and Denmark. It was our great delight to watch their enjoyment as our favor with the airlines allowed them to be upgraded to first class. In fact, it seemed everywhere we traveled we were blessed with several types of upgrades, causing them to exclaim, "We're never going anywhere without the Crones from now on!"

One last thought regarding favor. Jealousy and ingratitude will blind you to the favor you already have and block the continual increase of favor over you.

Being thankful for the favor that is extended to you and rejoicing in the favor of others, on the other hand, will position you to see and experience favor wherever you go.

As you make the following declarations, remember that you are a much-loved child, not a slave; a bride, not a beggar.

You are favored.

"Favor" Declarations

I DECLARE...

That God positioned me for favor through the cross.

I DECLARE...

That God has claimed me as His child.

I DECLARE...

That favor is a gift from my Father.

I DECLARE...

That as His child, I have favor.

Therefore:

I HAVE FAVOR...

To overcome any obstacle or difficulty.

I HAVE FAVOR...

To break through to breakthrough.

I HAVE FAVOR...

To take my enemies captive.

I HAVE FAVOR...

To resist the enemy and make him flee.

I HAVE FAVOR...

That breaks the yoke of oppression over my life.

I HAVE FAVOR...

To take vengeance on the enemy.

I HAVE FAVOR...

To step into my identity and destiny.

I HAVE PERMISSION...

To challenge my circumstances with the favor of God.

I HAVE THE FAVOR of God...

- In my passionate relationship with Him,
- On my family finances,
- Over my health,
- On my place of work,
- On my business,
- On my children, and
- On the prodigals.

We, as a community of believers, and all those in my household, live in a lifestyle of ongoing, never-ending, unprecedented, unparalleled, and ever-increasing favor.

My Declaration

Make your own declaration of God's favor that extends to every area of your life.

PB

"We are raising
the next generation of
God-lovers and
Kingdom-keepers."

—Tammy Hawkins

10 Children

Children are a heritage from the Lord. (Psalm 127:3)

Mark and Tammy Hawkins have been dear friends for many years. When I heard they were going to teach a class on "Praying For Your Children," I made sure my calendar was free in order to attend. Mark and Tammy have raised two great children, and the lessons they learned in the journey are real and full of wisdom. I entered the class with high expectation and was not disappointed.

One of Tammy's early statements quickly captured my

attention and stirred my own awareness of the immense responsibility—and privilege—of parenting.

We are raising the next generation of God-lovers and Kingdom-keepers.

Wow! Honestly, could there be any greater call than to be part of launching the next generation into their Kingdom destiny?

Tammy went on to talk about two essential elements in parenting: love and prayer. Though love is without question of primary importance, prayer, she stated emphatically, is also not an option.

Tammy continued, "The role of a parent is constantly evolving and changing as our children, circumstances, and life situations change. Likewise, our prayers and prayer strategies must also change right along with them. There may be a situation with our children, for instance, when God tells us to back away from direct involvement, but He never tells us to stop praying."

As I listened to Tammy, I was reminded that all the skills of parenting are important and certainly helpful in raising our children. Indeed, growing in these skills should not be ignored or left up to a casual approach. The same is true when praying for our children. In the busyness of our lives, we may not always communicate with them as we should or have the right answers for their seemingly incessant questions, and we often fail in our patience towards them. However, we must never neglect to pray for them. As parents, we are intentional about making sure our children take a bath, eat their dinner, and go to bed on time. We must determine to be just as intentional in praying for them.

Mark and Tammy concluded the class that evening with a crafted prayer based on several Scriptures. That prayer is at the heart of their new book, soon to be released, *Partnering With Heaven: Praying For Our Children*. Though the following is both petition and declaration, I have included it here because I believe it to be of such great value.

As we partner with the Holy Spirit for courage, insight, wisdom, and strategy in the huge task of raising our children, we can be sure that we are not alone in the task. He teaches us how to pray and exactly what to declare over their lives.

Tammy prayed the following prayer over the parents in her class, and I would like to pray the same in agreement with you:

> "Teach us, Holy Spirit, to pray what You want us to pray. Help us to see beyond what we see with our eyes. Give us eyes to see, ears to hear, hearts to understand, and courage, wisdom, and strength to do what You say."

Amen.

"Children" Declarations

Blank spaces are provided to allow you to personalize the declarations and petitions with your child's name.

Understanding and embracing our privilege and responsibility to pray for our children, we petition and declare the following:

We will not cease to pray for and make special request for

_____.

We ask that _____

- May be filled with the full, deep, and clear knowledge of spiritual things;

- May live and conduct himself/herself in a manner worthy of the Lord,

- May walk fully pleasing, and desiring to please Him in all things;

- May bear fruit in every good work, and

- Will steadily grow and increase in the knowledge of God with fuller, deeper, and clearer insight. (Colossians 1:9-10)

Father, we declare...

- The peace of Christ as the rule in _____'s heart, deciding and settling with finality all questions that arise in his/her mind. (Colossians 3:15)

- That _____ be subject to God and stand firm against the devil. (James 4:7-8)

- That _____'s determined purpose is to know You and become more deeply and intimately acquainted with You, perceiving, recognizing, and understanding the wonders of Your Person more strongly and clearly. (Philippians 3:10)

- That _____ may come to know the power flowing from Your resurrection and be fully in love with You all the days of his/her life. (Philippians 3:10)

Father, we are convinced and sure of this very thing...

- That the good work you began in _____ will continue until the day of Christ—right up to the day of Your return—bringing that good work to its full completion. (Philippians1:6)

- That _____ will learn to sense what is vital, and approve and prize what is excellent and of real value.

- That while knowing the moral differences, _____ may be untainted, pure, unerring, and blameless, and may approach the day of Christ, not stumbling, nor causing others to stumble. (Philippians 1:10)

- That _____ will walk in the fullness of the joy of the Lord all the days of his/her life and find that joy to be his/her strength. (Numbers 8:10)

- That You will show _____ the path of life and the way into Your presence where there is fullness of joy and everlasting pleasures. (Psalm 16:11)

- That You cause all grace, every favor, and earthly blessing to come to _____ in abundance, so that he/she may always—and under all circumstances— be furnished in abundance for every good work. (II Corinthians 9:8)

- That _____'s confession is he/she loves You fervently and devotedly, that You are his/her strength, rock, fortress, and deliverer; he/she will trust in, take refuge in, and call upon the name of Jesus and be saved from all enemies. (Psalm 18:1-3)

- Over _____, I speak prosperity and good health in body, spirit, and soul. (II John 2)

- That You have not given _____ a spirit of fear, but he/she walks in a spirit of power, love, with a calm and well-balanced mind, disciplined and self-controlled. (II Timothy 1:7)

- That _____ does not fret or have anxiety about anything, but in everything by prayer and petition with thanksgiving, makes his/her desires known to You. We declare that in so doing, Your peace will guard his/her heart and mind in Christ Jesus. (Philippians 4:6)

- That _____ has strength for all things in Christ who empowers, and is therefore ready for— and equal to—anything through Jesus who infuses _____ with inner strength. (Philippians 4:13)

My Declaration

Make your own declaration and petitions for the children God has given you.

Appreciation and value
for the differences in
each other
are essential for unity
to be authentic.

Unity

Make every effort to keep the unity of the Spirit through the bond of peace. There is one body and one Spirit— just as you were called to one hope when you were called. (Ephesians 4:3, 4, NIV)

In many denominational circles, unity is a straightforward issue: sameness. In other words, adopt the same doctrine, present the same look, and talk the same talk. This, in my opinion, is uniformity, and does not describe true unity. Having a value for uniformity ultimately requires that we gather around our sameness and separate ourselves from any other group or individual that has a different viewpoint or expression. The ultimate manifestation of the denominational spirit is this: if you disagree with me, I cannot accept you as part of the Body of Christ.

This really puzzles me. Why would we, as the church, adopt such a divisive stance? Paul made it very clear in the book of Ephesians that our oneness—or unity—is not in our agreement in doctrine, but rather, it is in our life in Christ. Our unity as a Body is not a common look, but a common Father who makes us all part of the same family. In fact, Paul is straightforward in his contention that we are already one, being united in one Spirit; therefore, our responsibility is not to create unity, but live in its reality.

> *As a prisoner for the Lord, then, I urge you to live a life worthy of the calling you have received. Be completely humble and gentle; be patient, bearing with one another in love. Make every effort to keep the unity of the Spirit through the bond of peace.*
>
> *There is one body and one Spirit— just as you were called to one hope when you were called—one Lord, one faith, one baptism; one God and Father of all, who is over all and through all and in all.* (Ephesians 4:1-6, NIV)

I am also puzzled as to why we are so adverse to difference. When I chose to ask Deborah to marry me, it was not because she was like every other woman in the world, but because she was unique from every other woman on the planet. I did not choose her because she was just like me, but because she completed me with her difference. I declare, "Vive la différence!"

It is my firm conviction that true unity is only possible through diversity. Appreciation and value for the differences in each other are essential for unity to be authentic. Division is not more than one vision, but a lack of value for the unique vision of another. Paul bears this out when he uses the function of the human body as an illustration of the Body of Christ.

> *Just as a body, though one, has many parts, but all its many parts form one body, so it is with Christ. For we are all baptized by one Spirit so as to form*

one body . . . God has placed the parts in the body,
every one of them, just as he wanted them to be. If
they were all one part, where would the body be?
As it is, there are many parts, but one body. The eye
cannot say to the hand, "I don't need you!" And the
head cannot say to the feet, "I don't need you!" (1
Corinthians 12:12, 13-15, 18-21, NIV)

One of the greatest joys of being a part of Christ's church in
our city is the fellowship we have with the other local churches
and their leaders. Some of my dearest friends are the pastors
of those differing expressions of the Body of Christ that occupy
Vacaville. An interesting thing about our unity is that we do not
agree on all elements of doctrine or theology. In fact, if we were
to delineate our beliefs and the unique way we have chosen to
live them out, we might discover that we have very few things
in common. It seems to me, however, that highlighting such
distinctions would be a waste of time and an exercise in futility.
Instead, we have chosen to value our unique expressions of
faith, and focus on the things we have in common. These alone
are enough, not only upon which to build friendships, but also
to connect us together in a strong bond of love and peace.

The greatest expression of unity I have ever experienced came
at a time when our differences within the church community were
at their greatest. At that time, The Mission was going through
a huge transition and experiencing manifestations of the Spirit
that were not only difficult to explain, but controversial as well.
Many people were uncomfortable with these varied expressions
of God's presence we were exploring and were leaving The
Mission. This caused many of the pastors in the community to
be concerned for our viability as a "true church."

In the middle of such intense and challenging circumstances,
friendship came from an unexpected source, the pastor of a local
conservative Baptist church. We could not have been farther
apart in what our congregational expressions and liberties looked

like, and our doctrine certainly stood apart from each other. Yet, it was this pastor, Milton Steck, who called and invited me to pray with him on Wednesday mornings.

I readily accepted Milton's invitation, and for several years, we met every Wednesday morning praying for our city, churches, families, and each other. We never questioned each other's theology or called into question our church practices; we simply shared our common faith and prayed. That invitation began a friendship that continues to this day, and the memories of our praying together are some of the richest of my twenty-plus years in this city.

We often take time in our services to pray over the many unique church expressions of our community. We typically pass out placards with the names of individual churches and have the congregation call out the names in prayer. One Sunday morning, Mark and Tammy Hawkins, leaders of our intercessory ministry, invited representatives from the local churches with whom we have the closest relationship to participate with us so we could corporately pray for them more specifically. A set of declarations were prepared that were the foundation of our prayer time. It was very exciting to have five churches represented on our platform as we all together made the following declarations over the Church of Vacaville.

I hope you find the following unity declarations useful and inspiring for your own community.

"Unity" Declarations

We thank You, Father, for the churches and the Body of Christ in Vacaville. Thank You for the men, women, and children who love You, worship You, and are committed to establishing Your kingdom in this city.

WE DECLARE...

That Your goodness, richness, and fullness will fill every church to overflowing.

WE DECLARE...

New life over the visions, dreams, and desires You have placed in their hearts.

Breathe fresh breath upon each one of them.

WE DECLARE...

Physical health, relational health, family health, financial health, and spiritual health to every church in Vacaville.

Teach us, Father, to function on deeper levels of love, kindness, wisdom, strength, and unity as we journey together.

WE DECLARE...

- Unprecedented opportunities,
- Doors wide open,
- Treasure chests unlocked, and
- Fresh divine adventures.

WE DECLARE...

- Unparalleled increase,
- Increased revelation,
- Increased community,
- Increased prosperity, and
- Increased God encounters.

TO THE CHURCHES OF THIS CITY, WE DECLARE that

- Your eyes will see,
- Your ears will hear, and
- Your hearts will continually comprehend what our Father has for you because He loves you.

May the LORD bless you and keep you.

May the LORD make His face to shine on you,

And be gracious to you;

The LORD turn His face toward you and

Give you peace.

(Numbers 6:24-26, NIV)

My Declaration

Make your own declaration that reflects your resolve to appreciate and value the diversity of the Church in your city.

Jesus came to reveal the Father
so we could experience Him and
enjoy ongoing communion through
His Spirit living in us.

12
Holy Spirit

The original life of the Father reproduced in His Son is the life the Spirit now conducts within us. (Romans 8:14, The Mirror Translation)

From the first chapter of Genesis to that last chapter of the book of Revelation there is one presence that dominates. He is the One that hovered over the face of the waters at creation, directed the glorious chaos of the day of Pentecost, interrupted Peter's speech by baptizing Cornelius, and He is the

One at the end of the Book who joins with the Bride in crying, "Come!"[20]

Throughout Scripture, we see His work in carrying out the will of the Father, empowering the Son, and inhabiting the believer. He is occasionally misunderstood, sometimes feared, and often ignored—even by those whose bodies house Him.

In case you have not figured it out, I am speaking about Holy Spirit. He is not an "it"; He is a Person—the Third Person of the Godhead. He is not a lesser God; He is God.

We often speak of Him as "the presence," and refer to how our inner man and our physical faculties manifest the reality of Him being with us. Right now, as I sit in my office working on this book, my spirit and body are resonating with His presence. I am reminded of a lesson I learned a long time ago: when you talk about Him, He loves to make Himself known.

Several years ago my dear friend and colleague Dan McCollam traveled with me to the interior of China. We secretly met over a two-day period with a group of Chinese believers in an apartment. Being discovered by the police in that setting would be inconvenient for us but especially harmful to those believers. In order to protect them, Dan and I taught the entire 8-hour sessions each day in a whisper.

On the first morning of teaching, I traced the work of Holy Spirit throughout the Scripture. About halfway through the teaching, we began to notice that Holy Spirit was not so interested in keeping things as quiet as we were. While I whispered passages about Holy Spirit, the students began to be overwhelmed by Him in response—joy and laughter broke out in a not-so-quiet way. These believers had never before experienced this particular manifestation of joy, and we had not even suggested it.

---

[20] Revelation 22:17.

We became very concerned, quite honestly, at the rising intensity of their vocal response and moved among them to quiet them, for their own safety. This only made the situation worse. The more we laid hands on them, the happier they got! At this point, we simply prayed God's protection over us all and trusted what Holy Spirit was doing.

When you talk about Holy Spirit, He shows up—He manifests His presence.

In the year 2011, I preached a series of Sunday morning messages entitled "Experiencing God in 3D." The premise was simply that God has presented Himself as Father, Son, and Holy Spirit, and that we have been given access through the cross to experience Him in all three dimensions.

On the third Sunday morning, I took the first part of the message to slowly and deliberately read fifty-five descriptions of the Person of Holy Spirit. I gave full permission for people to expect an experience with Holy Spirit even as I read through the descriptive declarations of who He is. They took that permission seriously, and Holy Spirit did not disappoint.

We are possessed, and we do hear voices. Jesus did not come to give us a book about God. He came to reveal the Father so we could experience Him and enjoy ongoing communion through His Spirit living in us. The Father is God *for* us; Jesus is God *with* us; and Holy Spirit is God *in* us.

> The original life of the Father reproduced in His Son
> is the life the Spirit now conducts within us (Romans
> 8:14, The Mirror Translation).

As you read through the following declarations, you have a choice: get an education or have an experience. I encourage you to give yourself permission to have an encounter with God through His Holy Spirit. You will not be disappointed.

"Holy Spirit" Declarations

He is:

- The Spirit of God
- The Spirit of Jehovah
- The Spirit of Christ
- The Spirit of the Father
- The Spirit of promise
- The Spirit of holiness
- The Spirit of truth
- The Spirit of wisdom and understanding
- The Spirit of might and counsel
- The Spirit of knowledge and of the fear of the Lord
- The Spirit of grace
- The Spirit of glory

He is:

- The indwelling Spirit
- The comforting Spirit
- The convicting Spirit
- The convincing Spirit
- The eternal Spirit
- The regenerating Spirit
- The same Spirit who raised Jesus from the dead

He is:

- The distributor of the love of God
- The imparter of life
- Our personal intercessor
- Our leader
- Our guide
- The teacher of truth
- The revealer of truth
- The guide to and in truth

He is:

- The fire of God
- The anointing
- The oil of anointing
- The oil of gladness
- The oil of healing
- The seal of our salvation
- The down payment of our eternal inheritance
- The guarantee of every blessing

He is:

- The gift-giver
- The gift of the Father
- The promise of the Father
- The rivers of living water
- The descending dove

- The Ruach—the breath and wind of God in the Old Testament
- The Neuma—the breath and wind of God in the New Testament

He is:

- The overshadowing that produces life
- The inspiration that authored Scripture
- The inspiration of Scripture
- The voice of God
- The power of God
- The everywhere-presence of God

He is:

- The witness to our adoption
- Our baptizer into Jesus
- Our baptism from Jesus
- Our liberator
- Our impartation
- The divine One

He is Holy Spirit.

My Declaration

Make declarations that come out of your personal journey with the Holy Spirit.

God invites us
to participate with Him
in a lifestyle of the
miraculous.

CONCLUSION

I believe you would agree with me that God can do anything He chooses to do. After all, He is God. He lacks nothing, is not on a budget, and asks no one for permission. However, He has chosen to partner with us to bring His will to manifest on this Earth.

Imagine with me what the disciples must have thought when they approached Jesus about the need to feed a crowd of more than 5,000 hungry people and His response was, "You feed them!" It must have sounded like a joke, or at the least a misunderstanding. It was neither; Jesus was inviting them to participate in a miracle through a divine partnership.

Ezekiel was a little unsure of what his response should be when God queried him about a valley of dry, dead bones, "Son of man, can these bones live?"[21]

---

[21] Ezekiel 37:3, NIV.

His reply, "O Lord...You know!"[22] must have seemed like the safest thing to say in the moment. Here again, God was extending an invitation for Ezekiel to partner with Him and declare the word of the Lord so that life would come where death reigned. "Son of man, can these bones live?" was not so much a question to the prophet that required his correct answer, but rather, it was God's offer to participate with Him in a miracle.

As you have read through this book, it is my desire that you have heard the invitation from Heaven to partner for breakthrough by way of intentional declarations.

Jesus instructed the multitude to hear His call and heed His words:

> He who has ears to hear, let him hear. (Matthew 11:15, NIV)

It is also my hope that your partnership with God will not be a singular event, but rather, a lifestyle of proclaiming truth in a way that establishes the will of God for you, your family, and the world around you.

---

[22] 37:3, NIV.

ABOUT THE AUTHOR

David Crone and his wife, Deborah, are the Senior Leaders of a community of believers called The Mission in Vacaville, California. They have been in full-time vocational ministry for over 40 years and have served at The Mission for over 20 years. While at The Mission, they helped transition a local church into a global ministry that provides resources for their region and the nations. Their value for team ministry has developed a culture of strong leaders, some of who serve with David and Deborah on the core leadership team of The Mission. Their lives and ministry are known for authenticity, a passion for God's presence, and a pursuit of His kingdom on Earth.

David is a director of Deeper School of Supernatural Life, a ministry of The Mission, and, along with Deborah, serves on the teaching staff of the school. They also are part of the Global Legacy apostolic team that oversees a growing number of churches in partnership for revival.

In partnership with The Mission, Mark 16:15 International, and Kingdom Development Group of Australia, David has developed supernatural training schools in the Philippines and Fiji. These schools train believers in releasing Heaven on Earth through personal transformation and signs and wonders. He serves as the International Director of Mission Fiji and Deeper Life, Philippines.

David has traveled extensively, ministering in 21 nations. He is also the author of three books. Deborah, an accomplished artist, has her paintings in the galleries of two of the largest art cultures in the world: Napa Valley in California and Maui, Hawaii. David and Deborah are welcomed speakers at conferences and churches, both at home and abroad.

RESOURCES

For more

resources from

David Crone,

visit The Mission Bookstore

online at:

iMissionChurch.com

Also available at:

Amazon.com

DaveCrone.com

More Books by David Crone

The Power of Your Life Message
Foreword by Bill Johnson

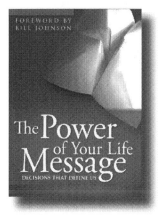

Author David Crone shares his deeply personal journey which brought him into an intimate relationship with His heavenly Father. You will be challenged to change your mindset, which then opens the door to internal transformation. You will learn how to define your life message and how to make decisions that lead to fulfilling God's exhilarating and exciting plans for your current and eternal destiny.

Book (236 pages): $15

Decisions That Define Us
Foreword by Bill Johnson

In *Decisions that Define Us*, David Crone documents his personal and corporate journey of transformation as Senior Leader of a transitioning church in Northern California. Each decision in this book represents the spoils of a battle fought and costly Kingdom lessons learned by this leader, his team, and their local fellowship. Within the pages of this book, you will be challenged and inspired to pursue God's kingdom at any cost and to discover practical ways of expressing the supernatural in your own life.

Book (130 pages): $11

Audio CD Resources

Four Questions to Destiny
David Crone

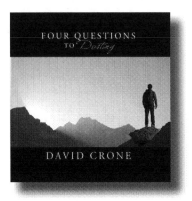

We are redeemed people with a redemptive nature and assignment: to be Christ's redemptive grace to a broken and lost world. In this message, David asks four important questions that will draw you into the mission that can transform the world around you.

Audio CD (1): $10

Living Larger than Life
David Crone

We all live under pressure, but it's the privilege of every believer to live larger than the constraint of their circumstances. In this 4-CD series, David Crone addresses small and restrictive mindsets, reveals perspectives that enlarge the inner man, and illustrates an essential element to living large under pressure and in the storms of life.

Audio CD (4): $30

No Hanging Harps
David Crone

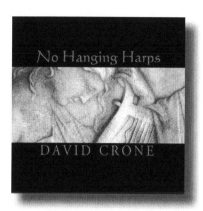

The tragedies and crises of life can leave us ready to give up and walk away from our destiny. In "No Hanging Harps" you can find the courage to turn those times into declarations of purpose and hope.

Audio CD (1): $10

More than Enough
David Crone

The measure of the Kingdom is fullness. The generosity of its King is exceedingly, abundantly above all we could ask or think. "More than Enough" will open the heart of the listener to live in the world of God's abundance.

Audio CD (1): $10

Experiencing God in 3D
David Crone

The three-session CD set.

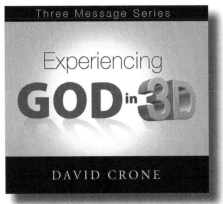

God has revealed Himself as Father, Son, and Holy Spirit so we can experience Him in every aspect of His nature and character. No matter how long we have known God, we may be living in only one or two dimensions, but not in the fullness of all three. This series explores what's available when we experience God in all three dimensions.

Audio CD (3): $25

When God says Enough
David Crone

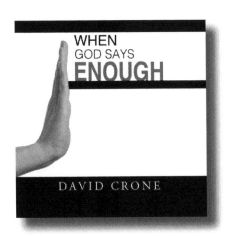

Got trouble? Being harassed? Facing intimidating circumstances? Is life not making sense? Does the attack seem relentless—never-ending? It's time for God to arise and say, "Enough!"

Audio CD (1): $10

Life of Discovery
David Crone

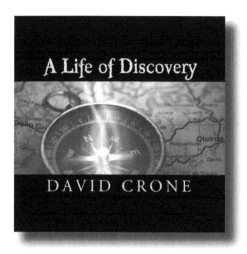

Each aspect of God's character and nature is an eternal adventure of its own. In this message, you can find the places God has hidden transforming revelation for you to discover.

Audio CD (1): $10

Shopping in the Presence
David Crone

In this message David Crone walks the hearer through nine stores in the Mall of His Presence, where there is no limitation of supply: the more you need, the more you can have. Every store is filled with good and perfect gifts. "Shopping in the Presence" is more than a message; it's an experience.

Audio CD (1): $10

35507357R00082

Made in the USA
Middletown, DE
10 February 2019